better together*

*This book is best read together, grownup and kid.

 akidsco.com

a
kids
book
about

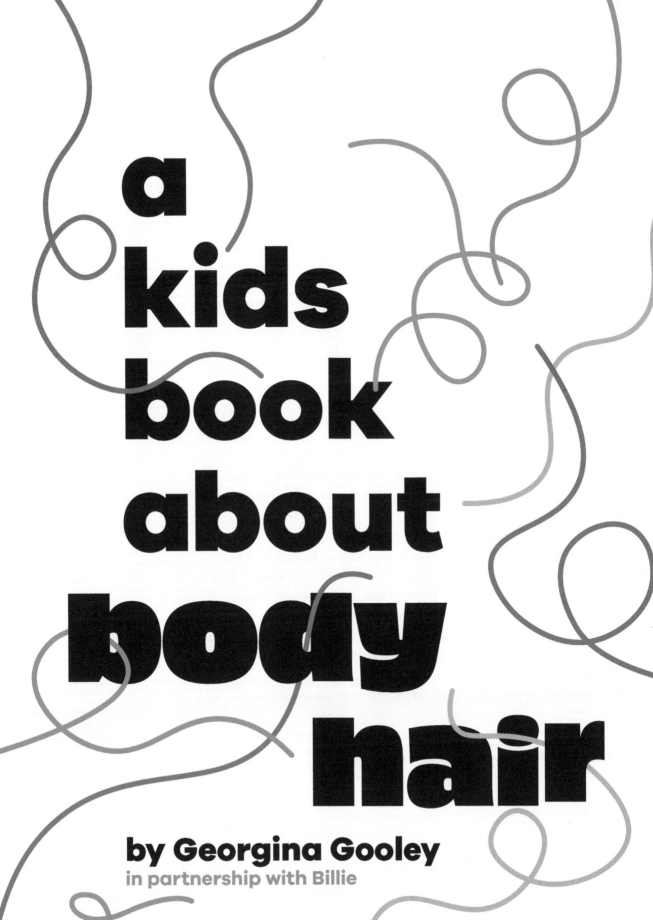

a kids book about body hair

by Georgina Gooley
in partnership with Billie

a
kids
book
about

Printed in the United States of America.

A Kids Book About books are available online: *akidsco.com*

To share your stories, ask questions, or inquire about bulk
purchases (schools, libraries, and nonprofits), please use
the following email address: *hello@akidsco.com*

ISBN: 978-1-953955-72-2

Designed by Gabby Nguyen
Edited by Emma Wolf

This book is dedicated to the humans
big and small who have body hair...and maybe
aren't quite sure how to feel about it yet.

Every time you revisit this book, we hope you
discover new things about your body and
love how special it is—hair and all.

Intro

When it comes to body hair, almost everyone has it—but not everyone likes it. This book aims to change that, helping kids create positive connections to their body and hair, so their first associations are ones of discovery, normalcy, and maybe even a little bit of pride.

Openly talking about body hair also allows grownups to consider their own relationship with body hair and the messages they send about what hair is acceptable on which bodies. We know it'll take more than a book to change cultural ideas around body hair, but teaching kids that body hair is pretty cool (before society tells them otherwise) feels like a good place to start.

This is a book about

boo
a
n

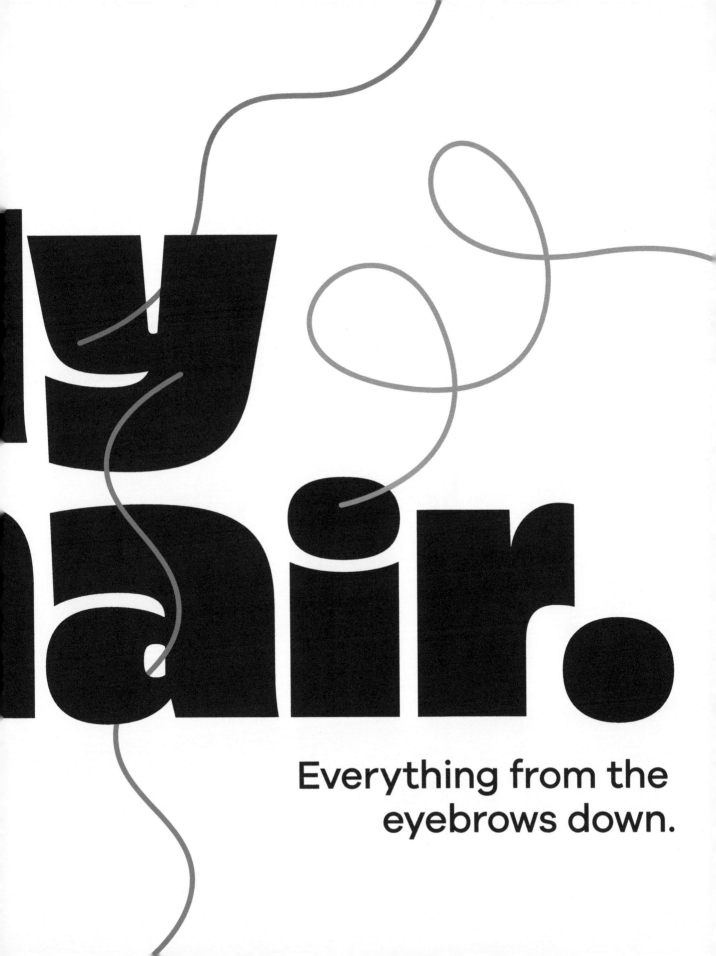

ly
hair.

Everything from the
eyebrows down.

If you look closely, you'll find hair almost everywhere on your body.

On your toes,

in your ears,

in your nose,

on your stomach,

and even little hairs
on your knuckles.

Surprise!

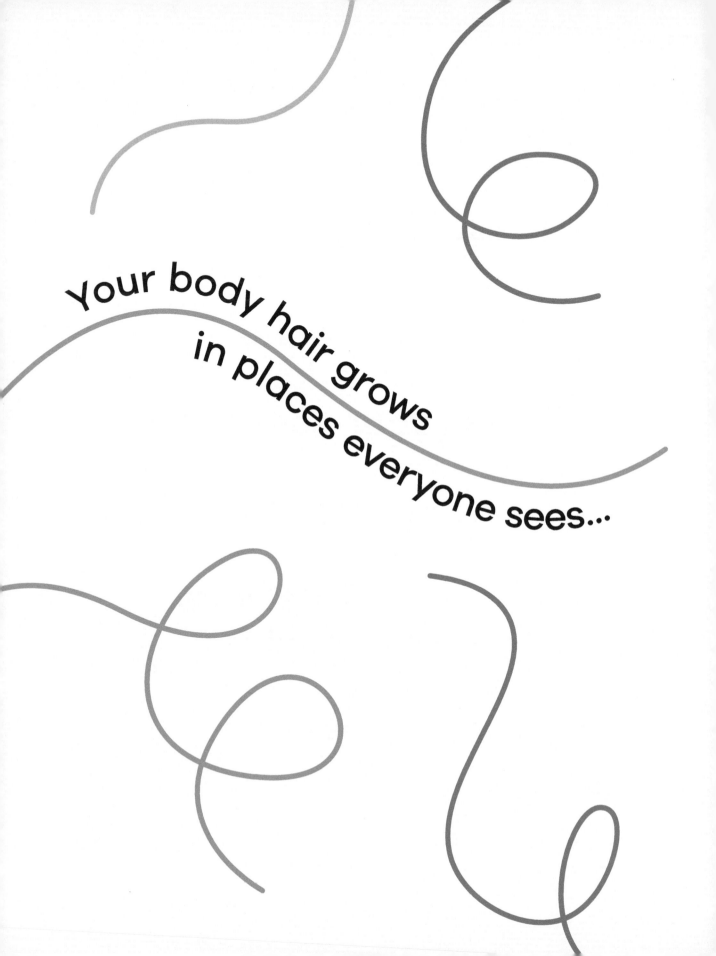

Your body hair grows in places everyone sees...

and in places only you can see.

Day by day, hair changes too.

It might look darker, feel thicker, and start to grow in different places.

(Yep, even in your armpits, on your butt, and around your private parts.)

It might look **different** from the hair other people have too.

Body hair comes in all kinds of colors and textures.

It can be...

coarse

wispy

bushy

thin

black

blonde

and SO much more!

You never know when or where it's gonna show up.

Some of your friends might get hairy armpits before you do, or way after.

Hair grows at its own pace, so just let it do its thing.

Your body hair has lots of important jobs to do every day.

It helps protect sensitive areas of your body, sweeps dust out of your eyes, and even keeps you warm.

You're born with hair as a baby and use it every day of your life.

It's a really cool part of being human!

Look down at your arms or legs. Can you see any little hairs?

They might be small or soft or hard to see, but they're there!

What do they remind you of?

How do they feel?

The truth is, pretty much all humans have body hair.

This means almost everyone you know has some!

Your favorite teacher has it (your least favorite teacher has it too).

The people who deliver your mail and your pizza also have body hair.

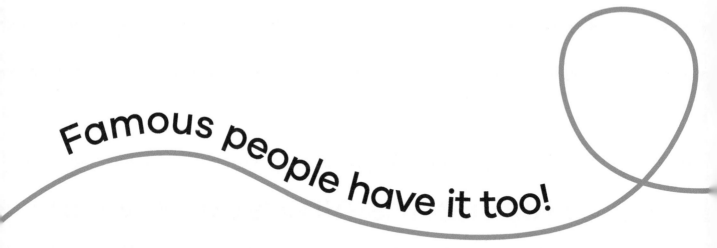

Famous people have it too!

Abraham Lincoln grew a bristly beard when he ran for president (they're also called whiskers).

Frida Kahlo was a painter with powerfully bushy eyebrows that came together in the middle (sometimes called a unibrow*).

Some movie stars and singers even show off their armpit hair on the red carpet. So fancy!

*Uni means one!

Is there anyone who doesn't have body hair?

For sure!

Some people lose their hair (it falls out) when they get very sick.

Some people are born without a hair gene and they never grow hair anywhere, even on their heads.

Our bodies all do different things—**there's no one way that fits everyone.**

Yours might look different from the hair other people have too.

People don't really get to choose if and when they grow body hair,

but we ca

what to d

n choose
o with it!

Some people like to keep their hair just the way it is, **100% natural.**

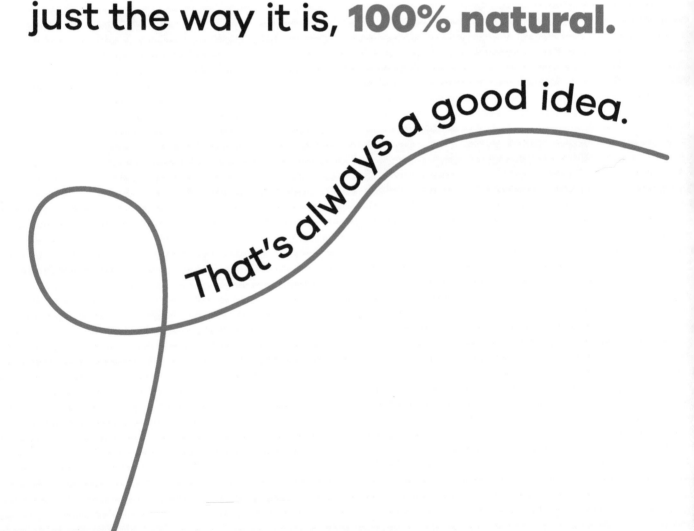

That's always a good idea.

Some people like to **remove it,** just to see how it looks.*

How do grownups remove hair? They might shave with a razor, pluck with tweezers, apply wax and strips, or use a special hair-removing cream. There's even something called "sugaring."

*Until you're a little older, please talk with a grownup before making any hair removal choices on your own.

Removing your body hair isn't permanent—your hair always grows back afterwards.

This means you can try out new things and if they don't work out, no problem.

There are lots of reasons people might remove their body hair.

Maybe that's how their family does it.

Maybe they're athletes who want to feel fast and strong.

Maybe they like the feeling of smoothness.

Maybe their friends are trying it, and they want to fit in.

But, wait a second. If it's normal to have body hair, why would removing it help you fit in?

Well, a long time ago, someone decided what **"the rules"** of body hair should be.

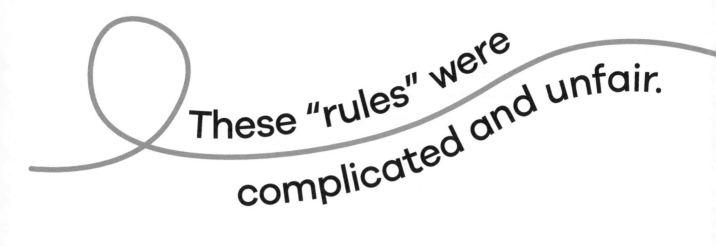

These "rules" were complicated and unfair.

For example, men could let all their body hair grow naturally. They only needed to shave their faces...if they wanted to.

Today, a lot of men
still enjoy the natural option,
but there are plenty who like
smooth legs and shaved armpits.

Sometimes men even wax
their chests and backs.

Anything's on the table!

Women used to have a lot more "rules" to follow.

For so long, women felt pressured to remove almost all their body hair (what?!), especially on their legs, armpits, and sometimes arms.

Mustaches and fuzzy bellies were a definite no-no.

Why would so many of us pretend we don't have body hair?

Why would the "**rules**"

be different for different people?

Today, people are ditching these old rules and deciding things for themselves, day by day.

Because no one person gets to decide how all hair should be.

If you're reading this with a grownup, ask them if they remove any of their body hair.

Why do they do it?

Have they always done it that way?

There might be a time
when someone asks about
your body hair.

There might be a time
you are curious about
the texture or color of
someone else's hair.

It's normal to have questions.

It's also important to be extra careful not to hurt anyone's feelings or use negative words for their hair.

Remember, body hair is never:

too long, too short, too dark,
too thick, in the wrong place,
smelly, gross, ugly,
or anyone else's business!

Body hair is always:

part of your heritage and history,
there for a reason,
with you wherever you go,
and pretty cool-looking too!

If you ever want to ask questions about someone else's body hair, **ask them** if they want to talk about it first.

What happens if you meet a person who says body hair is bad or gross?

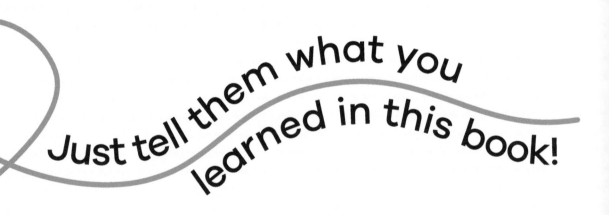

Just tell them what you learned in this book!

You can say:

"Nope, I love my body hair."

"Body hair is natural.
You have it too!"

"If you learn more about
body hair, you'll realize
it's not a bad thing."

"How can it be wrong
if everyone has it?"

Remember:
There are no rules about body hair.

Your body hair is an important and positive part of who you are—never forget that.

It belongs to you, and you get to choose what to do with it!

You and your hair have a lot to look forward to together.

In the meantime, just enjoy the way your hair is right now.

You don't need to change a thing!

Outro

You're never too young to feel good about your body hair—or too old either.

Kids, keep the conversation going by asking a grownup you trust any lingering questions you may have.

Grownups, share some of your own experiences through the years (both positive and negative), and be willing to explain the body hair choices you still make today. It's good to be honest! There's no need to hide if you felt mocked or pressured into removing your body hair—most of us did. Think about how old you were when you learned "the rules" of body hair and how long it took you to seriously question them. And if you started questioning literally this second, that's OK too.

a kids book about **MONEY**
by ...rumwasser

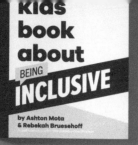
a kids book about BEING **INCLUSIVE**
by Ashton Mota & Rebekah Bruesehoff

a kids book about **diversity**
by Chernale Gordon

a kids book about **LEADER SHIP**
by Orian Jean

a kids boo abo **IMMI**
by MJ Calder

a kids book about **SAFETY**
by Soraya Sutherlin, CEM
in partnership with JUDY

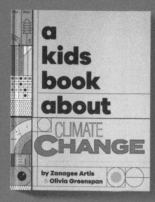
a kids book about **CLIMATE CHANGE**
by Zanagee Artis & Olivia Greenspan

a kids book about **IMAGINATION**
by **LEVAR BURTON**

a kids book about **GENDER**
by Dale Mueller

a k b a S
by Ev...

s ok out **IETY**
by ...hy Faces

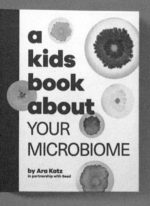
a kids book about **YOUR MICROBIOME**
by Ara Katz
in partnership with Seed

a kids book about **racism**
by Jelani Memory

a kids book about **DISABILITIES**
by Kristine Napper

a kid boo abo **bore**
by: KYLE ST...

a kids book about **DIVORCE**
by ...shley Simpo

a kids book about **cancer**
by Dr. Kelsie Storm & Sarah Porter

a kids book about BEING **TRANSGENDER**
by Gia Parr
in partnership with The GenderCool Project

a kids book about **DEPRESSION**
by Kileah McIlvain

a ki bo ab P
by Meir...

a kids book about **THE TULSA RACE MASSACRE**

Visit us at akidsco.com to discover more stories.